THE PRAIRIE SCHOOLHOUSE

FOREWORD BY TONY HILLERMAN   DRAWINGS BY VAN DORN HOOKER

THE PRAIRIE

University of New Mexico Press   *Albuquerque*

Schoolhouse

JOHN MARTIN CAMPBELL

Library of Congress Cataloging-in-Publication Data
Campbell, John Martin, 1927–
The prairie schoolhouse / John Martin Campbell;
foreword by Tony Hillerman; drawings by
Van Dorn Hooker.–1st ed.
p.   cm.
Includes bibliographical references (p.).
ISBN 0-8263-1659-X (cl).
ISBN 0-8263-1660-3 (pa)
1. Education–West (U.S.)–History.
2. Farm life–West (U.S.)–History.
3. Frontier and pioneer life–West (U.S.)–History.
I. Title.
LA230.5.W48C36 1996
370'.978–dc20   95-4357
CIP

Contents

TO THE MEMORY OF MY FATHER JOHN MARTIN CAMPBELL, PRAIRIE HOMESTEADER AND SCHOOLTEACHER

Foreword

Tony Hillerman

Jack Campbell's Photograph of Plum Valley School touched off an old memory. I am a child of the poorer part of rural Oklahoma. Restore the two privies which sit on opposite sides of Plum Valley School and replace the baseball backstop essential to such places and you have the Georgetown School of my own boyhood.

Since most readers today are too young (or from roots too urban) to imagine such schools, let me skip back about sixty years and recall Georgetown as it was in those years of the Great American Depression and the Dust Bowl.

Technically, it should have been known as Sacred Heart, the name of the post office in the little "general merchandise" store a stone's throw down the dusty sectionline road. But Sacred Heart was a Popish name. It had been put on the place by the Benedictine monks who followed the Citizen Band Potawatomi into their exile in Indian Territory. A handful of German and French-named Roman Catholic homesteaders had been attracted from the north by the church the Benedictines had built, but generally immigration into Oklahoma Territory had been from the old Confederacy—rock solid Protestants. Most of the folks in the area were Hard Shell Baptists. Sending their kids to a school named Sacred Heart would have seemed un-American, if not downright pagan. Thus the public school was called Georgetown, even though nobody seemed to know which George was being honored.

Some of the Catholic kids went there, and some walked up over the hill to St. Mary's Academy. While the Benedictine monks had given up on Sacred Heart and moved their own school to the county seat before I was born, the Sisters of Mercy still operated the Academy for Potawatomi, Seminole, and Sac and Fox girls and admitted some local farm kids. Thus I was denied a role in our great moment of glory. Awkward as I was, I would have played in a state championship baseball game. And since I would have given us a necessary ninth player, we would have won it.

In those days basketball was considered a sissy sport, football had not yet emerged as the state mania, and baseball was king of Oklahoma. Every crossroad had its team, and George-

town school in 1938 had a dandy. My Uncle Chris helped coach, and my cousins Nibs, Goober, and Larry Grove were all on the team. So was each and every male enrolled who was old enough to swing a bat. The team competed in the state-wide American Legion grade school baseball competition. In 1938 it won its way to the finals in Oklahoma City and to the championship game against Capitol Hill.

I can only guess at the number of boys in the pool of talent the Capitol Hill coach had to pick from—probably hundreds. At Georgetown that year, only twenty-nine kids sat in the south room where grades four through eight were educated. Of those sixteen were girls. Of the thirteen boys, one was down with malaria and one had broken his wrist in a hay baling accident.

If eleven against hundreds seems unfair, it's because you're unfamiliar with rural demographics of the 1930s. Out in the corn fields and cotton patches those depression years, people went to school when economics allowed. Classes started in mid-summer and shut down for such enterprises as plowing, planting, and cotton picking. Students came and went, depending on whether "roughnecking" jobs were available in the Seminole oil field or following the threshing crews. That led to a notable difference between city and country ball clubs.

The city players were all thirteen and fourteen, the cream of a swarm of eighth graders. Georgetown had only four eighth graders. But while the Georgetown right fielder was a puny fifth-grade ten-year-old who wouldn't have been considered as waterboy at Capitol Hill, the pitcher was a nineteen-year-old seventh grader (a cousin of mine), the first baseman was a Potowatomi oil field worker who weighed about 230 and was at least twenty-one, and everybody in the infield needed a shave every morning.

Georgetown swept its way to the finals with the little kids in the outfield untested because the city grade schoolers could not hit grownup college-level pitching. Their hurlers got easy outs with Georgetown's ten-year-olds but were terrorized by the elderly infielders. Thus Georgetown came to the championships and what in my mind was a showdown between past and future.

The Capitol Hill coach protested that the first baseman was well past twenty-one, then the legal age of maturity. Even though there was no rule against mature grade schoolers, he argued that the man should be disqualified in the name of common sense. The umps, all city folks, agreed. The first baseman was disqualified.

Georgetown had arrived at the city with only ten players. One had gotten into a brawl the night before and went home. So the coach fielded eight. He backed his second baseman deep, left right field open (had I been there, he would have used me), and began the game one player short. But Capitol had no better luck than anyone else hitting nineteen-year-old curve balls. After six innings, Georgetown led four to nothing. The Capitol Hill coach appealed again to the umpires and pointed to a clause in the rule book which described a baseball team as nine players.

The umps told the Georgetown coach to come up with another player or forfeit. Alas, alas.

In my mind that decision is representative of what paved roads, telephone lines, the growth of cities, and the death of small farms has done to America. Jack Campbell set out to photograph abandoned schools, but he has given us a haunting portrait of our past. It was poor, if one measures poverty in material terms, but it was happy. And now it is forever dead.

Preface

The rural one-room school in which a teacher taught grades one through eight was to the children of the western plains the standard and often the sum of formal education. This little schoolhouse was a product of the Western Homestead Era, those years beginning late in the nineteenth century when the federally owned short grass prairies lying east of the Rockies, and the big sage country of the interior Northwest were opened to farming. But of the tens of thousands of homestead schools which eighty years ago dotted the western prairies, nearly all have disappeared, and most of those remaining have fallen to ruin. This book, based on a search for the few survivors, traces the life and times of the prairie schoolhouse.

The evidence presented here is derived primarily from traditional anthropological field techniques. Beginning in the summer of 1991 our search for the prairie schoolhouse covered much of the old, western homestead lands, including appropriate parts of fourteen western states. These archaeological surveys were followed by detailed examinations of sixty sites whose characteristics were recorded on standardized forms. And these data and their provisional interpretations were then reviewed and assessed in directed interviews with surviving homesteaders or their descendants.

The black-and-white pictures were taken by the author with a Crown Graphic view camera, and printed by Hugh N. Stratford from 4x5-inch Kodak Tri-X negatives. All photographs were made in natural light.

In addition to my editor, Dana Asbury, and to Tony Hillerman, Van Dorn Hooker, and Hugh N. Stratford, scholars instrumental in the creation of this book include Marjorie K. Shea, Melinna Giannini, Phil Ballard, Kenneth W. Karsmizki, D Ray Blakeley, Mari Lyn Salvador, Ian D. Wagoner, and Julie L. Jensen. Other important contributors are Jeanne Bachand, Howard Boggers, Donna J. Bunten, Donald M. Campbell, R. H. Dempsey, Virginia Glassburn, Wayne Fisher, J. Thomas Grissom, Barbara Hall, Chris Hedrich, Loren D. Horton, Quentin Indreland, Kenneth L. Kemp, Dorothy Kolling, Verna Lou and Wayne Landis, Raymonda and Toy McMillan, Joseph P. Maguire, Jim and Gayle Murphy, Odessa Shelden, Ivar Sondeno, Marsha Sweek, Lon Taylor, Marga Van Ommen, and Doris Whithorn. Many thanks to one and all.

THE PRAIRIE SCHOOLHOUSE

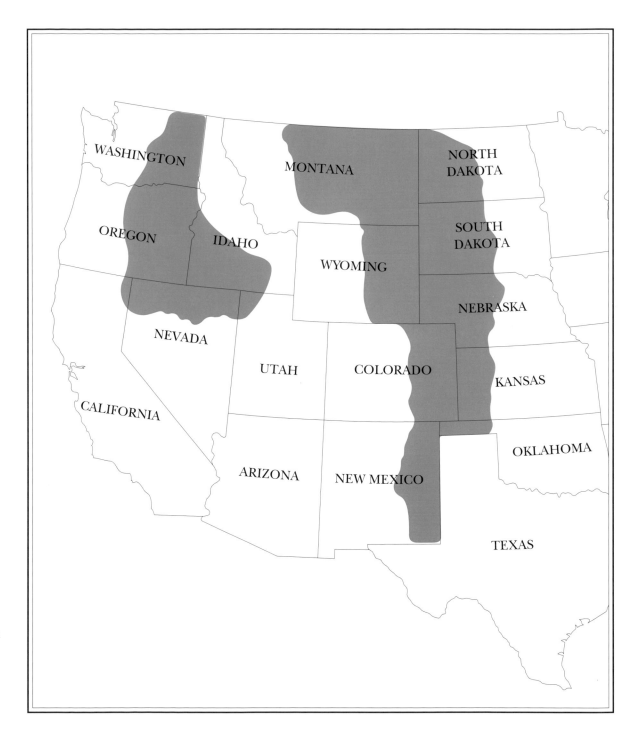

Lands of the Western
Homestead Era.

The Setting

The story of the prairie schoolhouse begins with the early years of the Western Homestead Era, the last grand episode in the opening of the American West. Homesteading, the formal process whereby a citizen could become owner of a piece of federal land, dates to a U.S. congressional act of 1862. It was legislation designed for the farmer, or would-be farmer, and, both in its provisions and restrictive scope, it was unique in the history of American land ownership.

Since the colonial period the European immigrant's thirst for his own plot of land was slaked by several means: armed conquest, expropriation, and Indian treaty or purchase being the most notable. Typically, these schemes involved a first possession by a corporate group or individual (the latter, the recipient of a crown grant, for example) who subsequently parceled out their domains among their kinsmen and followers. To name three of numerous examples, Manhattan Island, Pennsylvania, and the Valley of the Rio Grande thus became owned by invading white men.

But the Homestead Act of 1862 was something new. It catered to the farmer who was neither a member of an exclusive group, nor connected, nor wealthy, and it guaranteed a deed of ownership to any man or woman who met its requirements. These included: that the applicant be a U.S. citizen or had applied for citizenship; that he or she be twenty-one years old or the head of a household; that the applicant not own already more than 160 homestead acres within the state or territory in which application for "entry" was made; and that the applicant "file" only on a single piece of land containing a standard 40, 80, or 160 acres. (The latter, a "quarter section," one-fourth of a square mile, was by far the most popular unit applied for). Further stipulations were that in the first year of entry the applicant establish residence, that during the first three years he or she reside on the land for at least six months each year, that during the second year he or she cultivate at least one-sixteenth of the area entered, during the third year at least one-eighth, and that a habitable house be present on the land when "proof" was presented for title of ownership (after three years minimum, or five years maximum residence). Later, allowances were made in case of sickness, initial crop failure, or other pressing needs, but these were the central requirements. If all went well, in three to five years the homesteader became sole owner of his or her 40, 80, or 160 acres.

The most noteworthy early beneficiaries of the Homestead Act were people from the eastern and southern states who ventured out onto the open country of the central U.S. and who were the vanguard of farmers soon to create the Corn Belt. After the Civil War the American Indians who lived on these lush, tallgrass prairies—those who had not already died of white man's diseases—were driven onto reservations, and the oncoming homesteaders were free to settle and plough this richest of the earth's great farming regions.

The Western Homestead Era, however, was yet to come. Its farms were to occupy two immense reaches of western open lands: the shortgrass prairies of the Great Plains proper, which in the United States reach from the central Dakotas, Nebraska, Kansas, and Oklahoma to the eastern foot of the Rockies; and the sagebrush plains of the interior Northwest, including, mainly, large parts of Washington, Oregon, and Idaho. But in the twenty years or so following the Civil War, large-scale white settling of these lands awaited both access—via railroad—and the subjugation of Native tribes. The building of the big, transcontinental railroads, the Union Pacific, the Southern Pacific, the Northern Pacific and others, and the conclusions of the Indian Wars varied from place to place. But to choose, more or less accurately, an inaugural date for the Western Homestead Era, we shall pick 1885 as the year when the first homesteaders who rightfully belong to the era arrived on the western open lands.

They were hardly the first western farmers. Before them, between 1862 and 1885, a few homesteaders, taking their chances with potentially hostile Indians, had settled on river and creek bottoms among and beyond the prairies. Earlier, by the 1840s, farmers in the Sacramento Valley were taking their corn and wheat to trade at Sutter's Mill, Brigham Young and his followers were farming along the western front of the Rockies, and the Oregon Trail was leading many a Congregationalist and Quaker to clear and plow the enchanted valley of the Willamette. And even these settlers were latecomers to western U.S. farming. For there were the much earlier sixteenth-century Spanish farmers of the upper Rio Grande and, earliest of all, the Native Americans who, in modern-day New Mexico and Arizona, had been cultivating corn, beans, and squash for 2,000 years.

The above farmers are cited here for the sake of the record, but they and their ways of life can hardly be compared with those of the Western Homestead Era. The earlier white settlers were pioneers in the traditional sense of the term. They came on foot or on horseback or in covered wagons, and they clung to, or carved out, niches in a howling wilderness. They were "subsistence" farmers. They grew some of what they needed for food, bartered what surpluses they may have produced, and hunted, fished, and trapped.

And they were few in number. Before the Civil War, over any given fifty-year interval, all of the western farmers put together—native or white—had never amounted to more than several tens of thousands. Further, with few exceptions, the earlier farmers employed artificial irrigation systems of one sort or another. Most commonly, both Indians and whites settled in stream localities where, with the building of diversion dams and ditches, their neighboring fields were watered.

But in notable contrast, the planters and reapers of the Western Homestead Era typically came West by rail, practically overnight began producing market crops, over a span of some fifty years numbered in the several millions, and were nearly all "dryland" farmers. It is true that in the inaugural years they rode to town in buggies and wagons, and worked their fields with horses. And many of them hunted, fished, and trapped on the side. Still, the differences between the Homestead Era and earlier days of ploughing the West were of impressive proportions.

Overall, the single most telling, critical characteristic of the era's history—that which both resulted in its prosperity and caused its eventual ruin—was its "dryland" farming. Dryland farming is ages old. In the Western world it dates back well beyond the farmers and pastoralists of the Old Testament, and it means simply that in the absence of artificial irrigation systems the watering of domestic crops depends directly on falling rain or snow.

We have noted that practically none of the earlier western North American farming was dryland. Irrigation was necessary because without it the landscapes involved were too arid for crop growing. However—and perhaps surprisingly—from colonial times until the past few decades, most U.S. crops were produced without artificial irrigation. For example, depending upon the latitude, in that part of the U.S. that runs from the Canadian border to the Gulf of Mexico, and from 200 miles east of the Mississippi eastward to the Atlantic, direct watering from the skies will provide for practically any domestic crop .

But westward, across the shortgrass prairies to the foot of the Rockies and beyond, across the sagebrush country, the term dryland farming assumes a more critical significance. To cite a few comparative examples: at today's measurements, the country around Cedar Rapids, Iowa—the tallgrass prairie lands, now the heart of the Corn Belt—gets an average of forty-eight inches of annual precipitation, and south and westward, Topeka, Kansas, standing closer to the Rockies, gets thirty-three inches. But farther west, out on the old buffalo ranges, Clayton, New Mexico, gets fourteen inches; LaJunta, Col-

orado, twelve inches; and Glasgow, Montana, a little more than eleven. Across the Rockies, in the sagebrush country, Burns, Oregon, gets twelve inches, and Moses Lake, Washington, gets nine.

If you are a dryland farmer, forty-eight inches a year of combined rain and snowmelt is a bountiful abundance, and thirty-three inches is plenty, but at fourteen or nine inches you will grow neither corn nor wheat nor much of anything else. Yet the shortgrass prairies and the big sage country were the central defining focus of the Western Homestead Era.

Obviously, therefore, meteorological conditions must have been different then than now, and indeed, over much of the western regions, they were. In the 1880s and 1890s, and extending well into the twentieth century, typical localities on the western Great Plains were getting twenty or twenty-two or more inches a year. In agronomists' terms, such averages are somewhat marginal, but if they are sustained, and if only certain crops are attempted, they make for good dryland farming. So the homesteaders flocked in, and from eastern New Mexico to western North Dakota the buffalo grasses were ploughed under. At the same time, the sagebrush plains west of the Rockies were similarly settled. As it happened, however, the very low present-day precipitation levels cited above for eastern Oregon and Washington are close to those of the late nineteenth and early twentieth centuries. Thus, as we shall note further, farming on those dry lands was from the onset a losing proposition to thousands of Northwest interior homesteaders.

The Western Homestead Era coincided with arguably the single most telling event in the history of this country. At the beginning of the era the United States was notably underpopulated. For one thing, the recent Civil War had taken its toll of farm boys and men. And realizing that by natural increase alone it would take another century or two to fulfill its intended destiny, the U.S. loosened its immigration laws, most particularly those applying to non–English-speaking whites.

The resulting flood tide of immigrants numbered a total of nearly 16 million. An impressive fraction of them had been farmers in the Old Country—albeit, quite commonly, farmers of other peoples' property—who needed no instruction in the use of the plow, and once they disembarked on the eastern seaboard, they headed for the western prairies. Besides continental Europeans, the new arrivals in the West included immigrant Britishers and established U.S. farmers from the East, South, and Midwest, mainly of British and Pennsylvania Dutch (German) descent. As these English-speakers scattered out over the prairies they were instrumental in the promulgation of the language and in bridging the gap between European and American systems of government, law, and market.

As for the homestead lands themselves, the government

and the railroads advertised far and wide, as did private land locators who would meet their prospective clients at one or another western train station and show them around the countryside. But once western homesteading got rolling, letters to the people back home were most important in speeding the process of settlement. Glowing accounts of economic freedom (combined, naturally, with a persuasive urge to be with one's friends and kinfolk) emptied rural villages from Sweden to the Ukraine.

Countrymen settled with their own kind, thereby creating communities of ethnic and religious homogeneity. Over about forty linear miles in southwestern North Dakota the east-to-west lineup was German, Bohemian, Czechoslovakian, and Ukrainian, a pattern repeated across the prairies.

Overwhelmingly Christian, the homesteaders were accompanied or soon joined by clergy from the Old Country or "Back East." In the meantime, lay preachers filled in. While divine services were held first in any structure available (or in the open air), building proper churches was among the earliest priorities. Denominations ranged from Roman and Eastern Catholic to Lutheran and Southern Baptist, and typically, within three or five years after the first arrivals, domes or steeples marked the locations of the prairie settlements.

The wave of oncoming western homesteaders peaked in about 1915. It contained a total of three million adults who actually filed for homesteads, about one-half of whom eventually proved up (became owners). Twenty-five percent were women; between one-fourth and one-third were new European or British immigrants. As the immigration barriers had been removed, so now were the Homestead Act's provisions made more generous and attractive. Among continuing revisions, which varied from place to place, were those allowing more land per homestead, permitting teenagers as well as adults to file, and reducing the types and numbers of improvements necessary to obtain deed to the homestead. But noteworthy is that the stipulation requiring the applicant to reside on the property for a minimum of three years remained on the books; thus was permanent settling promoted and land speculation discouraged.

Not unexpectedly, there were shenanigans. As a group, land promoters and locators were more or less suspect. Some land speculators , while professing to be homesteaders, hired stand-ins to fulfill the residency requirement. And certain cattle and sheep ranchers, who had earlier preempted large expanses of federal land, persuaded their often numerous men and women employees to file on their pastures. The agreement, of course, was that once the homesteads were proved up the rancher would "buy out" the owners. Still, most of the homesteaders were honest. To the oncoming farmers, Old Country immigrants, Yankees, and Rebel soldiers alike, here was a new chance to make good.

The homestead combined subsistence living with, it was hoped, profit-making crops. On the typical homestead were the house (frame, stone, or adobe), the privy, a horse barn or shed, a chicken coop for fryers and laying hens, a pen for a hog or beef, and a kitchen garden. Except for the privy, all of the above depended on a windmill-powered well.

Beyond the immediate environs of the homestead headquarters lay the cash crop fields. Depending upon the current commodities markets and the meteorological qualities of the particular region, the main crop could be potatoes or corn, wheat or pinto beans. With any one of these crops, after two or three good years, you could go to the nearest big town like Rapid City or Amarillo and write a check for a new Studebaker wagon or Model T Ford.

Dirt roads, frozen solid as concrete in winter, and axle deep in mud or dust the rest of the year, tied the homesteads to their nearest town. But the lifelines were the railroads. While the smallest prairie settlement was likely to have a post office and a store, and as time passed, a gasoline pump, to be a real town you needed a railroad. Without a railroad, without a quick, sure way to get your crops to market, you could never be more than a bare subsistence farmer.

Thus, within a few years of its settling, each homestead region had a railroad track, or tracks. Some were main lines or branches of the big, transcontinental roads; others belonged to small, independent companies whose rails connected, eventually, with those of the big lines. Sometimes the towns came to the railroads, as it were, and in other cases the railroads were laid out to the towns.

Usually within the "city limits" of a real town there dwelt upwards of fifty or a hundred people, often several hundred. Always there was an eatery, church, hotel, bank, hardware, grocery, dry goods store, and stable or garage. Sometimes there was a high school and resident doctor, and commonly a saloon.

Homestead towns sprang up like mushrooms. Given the promise of a railroad, from unplowed prairie to full-blown town took typically one to four years. Selling town lots for homes, stores, and other establishments became a flourishing business. With an eye to developing the West, the states or the federal government awarded lands to rail companies, who in turn sold them to enterprising town builders. Or lots were bought, and towns developed from the owners of proved up homesteads.

And for ten, twenty, or forty miles beyond each town stretched the farms, dotting the prairies with their houses and barns and one-room schools.

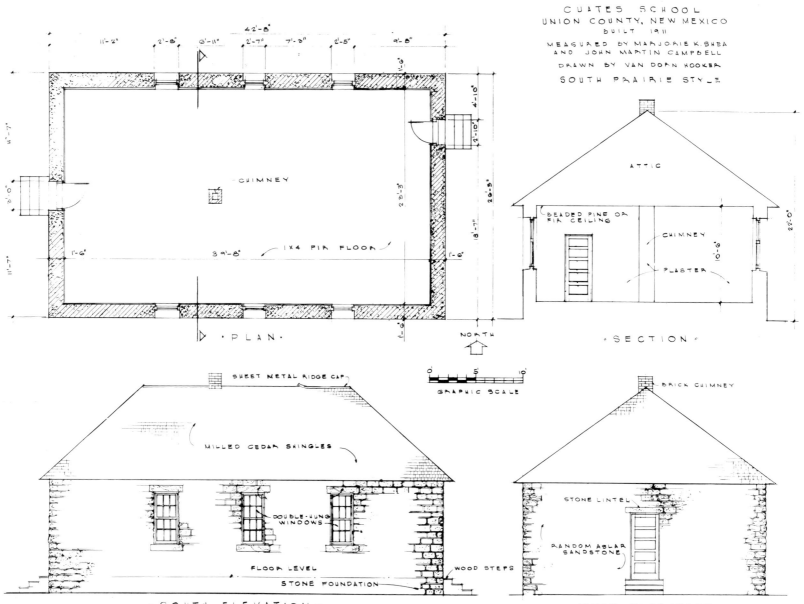

CUATES SCHOOL
UNION COUNTY, NEW MEXICO
BUILT 1911
MEASURED BY MARJORIE K. SHEA
AND JOHN MARTIN CAMPBELL
DRAWN BY VAN DORN HOOKER
SOUTH PRAIRIE STYLE

PLAN

CHIMNEY

1X4 FIR FLOOR

NORTH

SECTION

ATTIC

BEADED PINE OR FIR CEILING

CHIMNEY

PLASTER

GRAPHIC SCALE

SOUTH ELEVATION

SHEET METAL RIDGE CAP

MILLED CEDAR SHINGLES

DOUBLE-HUNG WINDOWS

FLOOR LEVEL

STONE FOUNDATION

WOOD STEPS

WEST ELEVATION

BRICK CHIMNEY

STONE LINTEL

RANDOM ASLAR SANDSTONE

The Prairie Schoolhouse

*I*t was an age when President Theodore Roosevelt (himself a descendent of non–English-speaking Dutchmen) was on the one hand welcoming aboard the tidal wave of immigrants, but on the other hand exhorting them to make English their language, and the sooner the better. That Roosevelt's advice went unheeded by some is a matter of record. Some immigrant women particularly, because it was the men who did business beyond the boundaries of home and church, never got around to learning the new language. But in both non–English-speaking and English-speaking families it was the women who were most insistent on the formal education of their children.

Many a homestead father grumbled when a child, needed on the farm, was at school instead. Some pupils attended school only three or four months a year, during slack times between harvest and planting. Nevertheless the children were sent to school.

The curriculum covered grades one through eight, all taught by one teacher. Overall, as we shall opine, the teaching was good to very good, even though according to modernist yardsticks, in the earlier decades of the era many of the teachers were hardly qualified to teach. In the early years, teachers included, among others, teenage eighth-grade graduates; high school graduates; college dropouts; men and women with baccalaureate degrees from schools such as Vassar and Maryville College; lawyers, accountants, and news correspondents, few of whom had ever taken an "education" course.

In the beginning, school was held in any shelter available, from cook tent to dugout, but excluding these early makeshifts, the typical prairie schoolhouse was patterned after the vernacular pioneer dwelling of northern North America. It was a simple, rectangular structure, with a pitched roof having a central ridge, either gabled at each end or hipped. This age-old design had its origins in the forests of northern Eurasia, perhaps in western Siberia, or the Scandinavian Peninsula. Long before the advent of the European Middle Ages it was common in Poland, Germany, the Low Countries, and the British Isles. Quite naturally, this dwelling style accompanied the seventeenth- and eighteenth-century Dutch, English, Finnish, German, and Swedish colonists to the American At-

lantic seaboard. Abe Lincoln's log cabin is a good nineteenth-century example.

The schoolhouse was homemade. Professional carpenters were scarce, and architects were practically unheard of, but most of the homesteaders had basic knowledge of carpentry and masonry, and some were expert amateurs who served as volunteer architects and contractors. Architectural variations resulted from builders' idiosyncrasies or their ethnic derivations. But the two major varieties of the prairie schoolhouse—those we may call the south prairie style and the north prairie style—were determined largely by climate, and the availability, or lack thereof, of construction materials.

On the southwestern Great Plains clayey soils are common, and sandstone or limestone bedrock is exposed in the cut banks of prairie creeks. Therefore, walls of both dwellings and schools were made of adobe or hewn stone blocks, topped with a low, hipped or gabled roof of pine lumber and cedar shingles. The adobe or stone walls were borrowed by the homesteaders from the old, Spanish-Mexican villages of the southern Rockies, where in turn they were derived principally from the architecture of the ancient Pueblo Indians. The low, hipped or pitched roof came with the railroads from the East. An unadorned front door and a similar side door near the back of the building opened directly on the schoolroom.

From the prairies of western Nebraska, north and westward, suitable construction stone is rare or uncommon, and the art of adobe building was unknown. Thus, of necessity, except for the earliest north prairie homesteaders (who commonly lived in rude dugouts), schools and other buildings were made of lumber, cut and milled in the Black Hills or other western ranges, and shipped by rail to the homestead market towns.

To shed snow the north prairie schoolhouse has a more steeply pitched roof than its southern counterpart. To ward off the cold it is distinguished further by being slightly smaller than the south prairie style. Additionally, it is characterized by double-hung windows set in outer and inner sliding sashes, a storm vestibule (an entryway having an outer and inner door), and the absence of a rear side door. In both styles, the schoolroom floor is elevated a foot or more above ground level, and the door is reached by one or more wooden, stone, or concrete steps.

Schoolhouse architectural details come in a seemingly endless variety, most of them decorative, and most of them occurring in the wooden schools of the northern plains. Departures from the usual north prairie style included interior cloakrooms, schools with two front doors, pyramidal roofs, hipped roofs with blind dormers, attic windows, and belfries. Few such embellishments accompanied the south prairie style, but structural variations included, uncommonly, schools made of wood or having walls of poured concrete or of stucco over wire mesh.

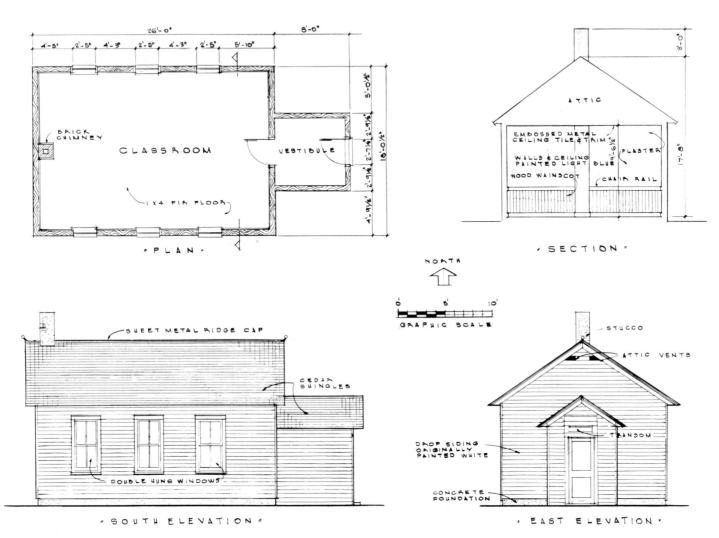

26'-0"   8'-0"

4'-5" 2'-5" 4'-3" 2'-5" 4'-3" 2'-5" 5'-10"

5'-0½"

18'-0½"

2'-7½" 2'-5"

4'-9½" 2'-9½" 2'-7½"

BRICK
CHIMNEY

CLASSROOM   VESTIBULE

1×4 FIR FLOOR

· PLAN ·

ATTIC

8'-0"

EMBOSSED METAL
CEILING TILE & TRIM

WALLS & CEILING
PAINTED LIGHT BLUE

WOOD WAINSCOT

PLASTER

CHAIR RAIL

1'-6½"

17'-8"

· SECTION ·

NORTH

0'   5'   10'
GRAPHIC SCALE

SHEET METAL RIDGE CAP

CEDAR
SHINGLES

DOUBLE HUNG WINDOWS

· SOUTH ELEVATION ·

STUCCO

ATTIC VENTS

TRANSOM

DROP SIDING
ORIGINALLY
PAINTED WHITE

CONCRETE
FOUNDATION

· EAST ELEVATION ·

MEYER SCHOOL
MEADE COUNTY, SOUTH DAKOTA

MEASURED BY MARJORIE K. SHEA
AND JOHN MARTIN CAMPBELL

DRAWN BY VAN DORN HOOKER

NORTH PRAIRIE STYLE

With or without variations, both north and south there were only minor differences in the size of the schoolroom itself and general uniformity in its arrangement and furnishing. The front of the room, containing the teacher's platform and desk, was in fact at the back of the schoolhouse, opposite its entrance. The teacher faced the entrance, while the pupils' desks, with a central aisle, quite naturally faced the teacher.

The teacher's desk occupied a low platform, elevated some eight inches above the main floor and the pupils. The platform reached across the width of the room, and from front to back measured about eight feet. On the wall behind the teacher's desk, or sometimes on a side wall, were slate blackboards. Again behind the teacher was a wall cabinet of large pull-down maps and often a standing United States flag. School books provided by the school district, parents, and public-spirited members of the local community were meant to be used mainly at school and were shelved on or near the teacher's platform. Always there was a wastebasket beside the teacher's desk, and on the desk top a hand-held school bell. A large, polychrome portrait of George Washington typically graced one of the side walls.

In the north, despite the elegant homemade designs of the buildings, winter heating of both dwellings and schoolhouses was a chronic, unresolved problem, a problem created by the nature of the outer walls. By necessity made of wood, they were ordinarily only seven inches thick, four inches of which was hollow interior. It may seem curious that the homesteaders, so many of whom were from northern climes, would build such flimsy houses and schools, especially in the face of plunging winter temperatures and howling blizzards. But both the farmers from the Old Country and those from the eastern U.S. were used to having better building materials, or had not had to cope with life on a barren steppe.

At home, with the cats under the cookstove and the dogs

scratching at the door, family winter life centered around the kitchen. Shut off from the rest of the house, and with outside air temperatures often dipping far below zero degrees Fahrenheit, the kitchen range was the sole source of heat for the household. Going to bed meant dashing upstairs and diving under a great pile of blankets.

School-room heating was provided by the traditional potbellied stove, which, fabled as it is in western farming and ranching lore, was a technological flop when it came to heating a north prairie schoolhouse. The stove stood on or near the teacher's platform, and within a few feet of the pupils' front row. The tin stovepipe, elbowed at a safe distance above the floor, led to the brick chimney built into the back wall behind the teacher.

The coal scuttle, replenished frequently from the coal shed out back, stood beside the stove which in turn was stoked throughout the day by either the teacher or a pupil big enough and smart enough not to get singed in the process. With outside temperatures standing at, say, minus 30 degrees Fahrenheit, a well-stoked schoolhouse stove would very nearly roast the front row of pupils, while those at the back of the room seldom took off their mittens. (In all fairness, this unhappy condition was only partly the fault of the stove. Southward, with winters far less severe, the potbellied stove worked very well within the thick stone or adobe walls of the classic south prairie school.)

The ground on which the school sat was acquired by various means. The federal government awarded to the states (or territories) in question so-called school sections, and in Colorado, for example, in each platted township of thirty-six numbered square miles, number thirteen was designated the school section. It was intended that somewhere on this square mile a schoolhouse would eventually be built, but of more practical importance was that the school section was meant to add to state ownership a potentially valuable piece of property which in future years could be sold or rented out.

A square mile contained considerably more ground than was needed for a one-room school; furthermore, in regions of intensive farming it was required that the schoolhouses be scattered no more than two or three miles apart. There were no school buses until "consolidation" reached the Western Homestead country, and pupils had to walk to school. (Consolidation was [and is] the practice wherein the prairie schoolhouses were abandoned in favor of multiroomed schools built in town.) The schools, therefore, were sited usually on an acre or two of land, donated by a homesteader with the understanding that if and when the school was abandoned, both it, its external structures, and its acreage would revert to the homesteader's possession.

Each prairie schoolhouse and its ground, was in effect an odd, small community unto itself, a place of unique endeavor, and its teachings, both practical and esoteric, illuminated homestead dwellings for miles in every direction. For example, in an age when tuberculosis, typhoid fever, smallpox, and diphtheria were scourges of young and old alike, the prairie schoolhouse was a dispenser of healthful wisdom and of doctoring as well.

The teacher's duties included keeping a wary eye out for rashes, head lice, impetigo, and pinkeye. Rashes were sent home; the others were treated on the spot. Both teachers and schoolbooks extolled the benefits of soap and water and proper clothing and diet. Among other cautionary or preventative examples, schoolbook drawings and texts explained how seepage from a misplaced privy could contaminate a cistern or well.

And these lessons were intended to be carried home. Numerous homestead parents were ignorant of health basics and downright hostile to some of them. During winter, the children of a few families were actually sewn into their long underwear, thereby preventing them from bathing for weeks or months at a time. And parents were often adamantly opposed to having their children vaccinated or inoculated, believing that the treatments were more deadly than the diseases.

We have noted that given the variety of teachers' talents, early prairie homestead education ranged from the sublime to the ridiculous. To improve on this situation, during the first two decades of the twentieth century, the western states, following their more eastern U.S. examples, legislated minimal teachers requirements. The requirements specified a two-year course of study at the college level, at the successful completion of which the student was awarded a certificate vouching for his or her capability to teach the lower grades.

Until the 1930s this salutary legislation sometimes went unenforced, but from about 1910 until the 1940s most teachers were being educated in regional, two-year colleges known as "normal schools." Each western state had several such normal schools, one or more of which was situated invariably out on the prairies. Thus, farm boys and girls who aspired to the teacher's life could earn their certificates without having to travel great distances from home.

The normal school's training was good. Its mission was clearly defined and not to be confused with the purposes of four-year colleges and universities which awarded baccalaureate and graduate degrees in a variety of professions. Rather, the normal school's faculty and administrators, with their bachelor's, master's, and occasional doctoral degrees, were dedicated to producing teachers of grades one through eight. Typically, their requirements and standards were demanding.

Throughout most of the era's history, a notable majority (60–80 percent) of prairie schoolhouse teachers were women, and most of them were young and unmarried. Her school belonged to a school district, administered most directly by a district superintendent who was hired by a school board whose members were elected by district voters. Depending upon the district's demography, the superintendent's domain included anywhere from six or eight, and up to fifteen one-room schools plus, commonly, an in-town high school. The superintendent was responsible ordinarily for the hiring and firing of the teachers (even though in 1910 one of this writer's favorite uncles, George Campbell, was fired on the spot for cleaning out the chairman of the school board in a poker game).

The power and directional authority of the board was fundamental, and within boundaries, the board was nearly autonomous and consisted of about five members (the author recalls three farmers, a store owner, and the cashier of a three-man, one-woman bank). The board reflected community mores which, if anything, were conservative and which incorporated straightforward attitudes regarding what belonged or did not belong in the curriculum, as well as school discipline, deportment, proper dress, speech, and the like. It was the

schoolteacher whose pay, depending upon time and place, ranged from three hundred to eight hundred dollars a year, who was expected to both live and teach this wisdom and virtue.

Most of the time she succeeded. Normal school training was rigorous, and the teacher tended to carry this quality of instruction out to the prairies. Keeping in mind that numerous homestead pupils would not go on to further schooling, the curriculum was designed to provide a "solid education" to everyone who graduated from the eighth grade. Core subjects included arithmetic, composition, geography, grammar, penmanship, physiology, reading, spelling and United States history. In addition, agriculture (for boys), and domestic science (for girls) were often included, as were civics, music, and drawing.

A suitable score on a grueling two-day written exam, would earn an eighth grade diploma. A typical eighth-grade examination, a 1912 Oklahoma example, contained about 140 questions, most of which would daunt a modern college student, let alone today's eighth grader. Here are seven of them: "Explain why colonial Massachusetts and Virginia adopted different forms of government; give the composition of the blood; give four rules for capitalization and punctuation; name six powers of congress; write sentences showing five uses of the noun; find the length of the longest straight line that can be drawn on a plane surface 16 feet by 10 feet"; and—hardest of all perhaps for today's fledgling feminist—"give two reasons why a girl should help with the housework."

At this late date it is impossible to assess with precision the effectiveness of prairie schoolhouse education. But on balance, on the scattered data available, one suspects that it was a good education rather than a poor one . The one-room school was, of course, bereft of audio visual apparatus, computers, grief counselors, career advisors, sex education, and school lunches, to name a few of several of today's essentials. Still, this schoolhouse turned out hundreds of thousands of literate teenagers who became functioning members of mainstream U.S. society.

Rightly and properly, the prairie school was designed to produce educated farm men and women, and they were its principal contribution to mainstream life. Tens of thousands of its graduates went on to careers in engineering, law, business, nursing, and other conventional professions. As for the oddball pupils—those who would rather be poets or paleontologists, and of whom there were quite a few—they had a solid early education. Among this writer's acquaintances are two distinguished historians with doctoral degrees from celebrated universities, whose careers were launched when, as six-year-old girls they were seated up front, in the "little seats" of one-room, homestead schools.

The End of the Era

To many of the homesteaders trouble came early. For a few, trouble was sheer, wide-eyed ignorance. These were urban men and women who, like the latter-day hippie commune dwellers, dreamed of the good life but hadn't the foggiest idea of what farming was all about.

For numerous others trouble was naiveté of quite a different kind. Most of the homesteaders were farmers in the first place; people from the Old Country or the eastern and southern states who were reared in regions, as we have noted, where artificial irrigation was usually unnecessary. In Connecticut, if you aspired to raising corn or pumpkins you cleared forest and hauled away boulders. Once that hard work was done, however, the rains and snows of New England watered your fields.

Compared to clearing New England trees and boulders, ploughing under sagebrush or shortgrass was a lark, but over much of the western prairies neither corn nor pumpkins nor practically anything else would grow without irrigation. Thus, many an otherwise sophisticated farmer went broke for lack of water.

Then, for many there was the problem of not enough land per farm. Overall, because on most of the western homestead lands little else would grow, wheat was to become the principal crop. But in general, profitable wheat growing required more than 160 acres, or even 320. Unless you could buy out your neighbors, or unless several members of the same family were old enough to file, you could not make a living growing wheat.

Finally, the markets fluctuated. While seed, horses, ploughs, and building materials were, at today's prices, ridiculously cheap, it still took a sizeable grubstake to get started. To reach your prospective homestead in the first place, build a liveable house (even a one-room shack), dig a well, and buy a team of horses, equipment, and groceries required a minimum investment of a thousand dollars or more. That was a lot of capital—all the capital available to many a homestead family. And if, as you were getting started, the bottom fell out of the

market, chances were good that you would lose your farm. Because of these kinds of discouragements there was from the beginning notable attrition.

Nevertheless, counting family members, several million dryland homesteaders made respectable livings. In Colfax and Union counties, and elsewhere on the plains of New Mexico, corn and milo maize provided for beef cattle and dairy farms, and with the coming of the First World War, broom straw was a paying crop. Pinto (navy) beans were even better; for more than three decades following the war, pinto beans supported dozens of south prairie towns. In eastern Wyoming, western Nebraska, and the western Dakotas, wheat, oats, barley, corn, potatoes, and hogs paid their way.

In part, this relative prosperity resulted from an increase in homestead size. In some regions governmental revisions permitted a land unit of 320 acres, or more. At the same time, both on the shortgrass prairies and in some of the big sage country, homesteaders with more capital than their neighbors were buying out those who wished to sell, or were buying abandoned homesteads for back taxes. Given a decent market, on the south prairies you could prosper on a square mile of pinto beans, or two or three square miles of wheat, and with wheat, in the north you could do the same.

The beginning of the end of the Western Homestead Era came with the stock market crash of 1929, followed closely by the Great Depression of the 1930s. If you are a farmer, you and your bank are partners in ownership. Even when you are doing quite well, each year you borrow ahead—for seed, machinery, and other essentials—on your next year's crop. Eventually, if all goes well you pay off your loans, or pare them down to where you are more or less self-sufficient. Meanwhile your bank holds as collateral your next year's crop, machinery, or possibly even the deed to your farm.

By 1934, early in the Great Depression, hundreds of west prairie banks had failed. Most of those that survived had little money to lend, or, facing dead markets, refused to lend it. Others foreclosed on their loans. Thereby, hundreds of thousands of homestead families went broke. Still, for other hundreds of thousands, the depression itself was not the worst of it. These were farmers who had become self-sufficient. They owed little money, if any, and they produced most of what they needed. With bartering, taking the occasional outside job, and the few dollars earned from selling produce, eggs, milk, or meat, they could weather through. A 1930s west prairie farm family, free of debt, could survive on $300 a year.

But by coincidence, the Great Depression was accompanied by the Dust Bowl, a phenomenon created by wind and prolonged drought. With some exceptions the farms it laid to waste were those of the Great Plains (the "Bowl"); most of the interior Northwest was unaffected. And while the Dust Bowl is associated usually with the 1930s, on some of the western prairie lands its winds were creating ghost towns as late as the 1950s. Drought was the primary factor. The homesteaders were accustomed to dryland living, weeks and months without rain or snowfall. But they had never seen drought like this. In the pinto bean regions, some farms went three and four years without a drop of rain. Wind did the rest, blackening the skies and burying fences in blowing topsoil.

The Dust Bowl has been blamed widely on the plowing under of prairie sod. Recent studies have shown, however, that over the past several thousand years, the interior West has endured several "Dust Bowls" whose causes had nothing to do with either prehistoric or modern farming practice. Rather, they have reflected climatic oscillations in, if anything, an increasingly arid environment marked by brief intervals of greater precipitation. And unbeknownst to either the homesteaders or the earth scientists of the day, the earlier years of the Western Homestead Era coincided with a relatively wet interval.

In any event, with the combined effects of the Great Depression and the Dust Bowl, by the early 1950s more than five million western prairie men, women, and children had been driven from their farms. Today, some of the abandoned homesteads are incorporated in big cattle ranches; some have come under irrigation; and others produce dryland wheat, now on farms of thousands of acres. But, for the most part, all that remain of the Western Homestead lands are scattered graveyards, ruined buildings, and the dim outlines of the fields—except for those millions of successful Americans, those graduates of the prairie schoolhouse.

Plates

PLATE 1.

Highland School, Douglas County, Washington, ca. 1900

☙

The old western homestead lands are immense. A far distant grain elevator can loom as your only landmark. In both their topography and their native plants, the prairies are close kin to the fabled Russian steppe, and indeed they are known as steppe to biologists and geographers.

PLATE 3.

Oregon Railroad and Navigation Company, Morrow County, Oregon, 1893

❧

Branch lines connected hundreds of small west prairie farming towns to the transcontinental railroads—the Southern Pacific, Great Northern, and others. And a welter of small rail companies were founded for the homestead trade. Thus, crops traveled to city markets, and in return came the necessities and desirables of homestead life.

PLATE 4.

The Best House in Sofia, New Mexico, ca. 1914

❧

Sofia, not surprisingly, was named and settled by immigrant Bulgarian homesteaders, farmers who ploughed under the buffalo grasses to become prosperous as growers of pinto beans. Within three years of its founding the town was being served by a prairie railroad, and had its usual, thriving commercial establishments. By the early 1920s it boasted a consolidated school.

PLATE 5.

Dining Room: Street Entrance, The Mt. View Hotel, Branson, Colorado, 1917

Every west prairie town served by rail had a two-story frame hotel. Upstairs were the ten or fifteen rooms. The lobby was furnished with a few overstuffed easy chairs, and a good, upscale hotel like the Mt. View had a dining room/saloon with both a lobby and street entrance.

PLATE 6.

Union County, New Mexico, date unknown

❧

As the era evolved, some homesteaders became sheep or cattle growers by either buying out their neighbors, or paying up back taxes on neighboring, abandoned homesteads. This barn was built to shelter livestock when "blue northers," the blizzards of the southern high plains, struck the Texas-New Mexico borderlands.

PLATE 7.

Unusual Homestead Residence, Quay County, New Mexico, ca. 1925

℘

The walls of this elaborate homestead dwelling are made of poured concrete. Its prosperity was generated by its basement facility with an imaginative apparatus that produced fifty-gallon barrels of prairie whiskey. But after a number of successful years the Bureau of Internal Revenue came out and ruined the whole enterprise—basement, upstairs, homestead, and all.

PLATE 8.

Homesteader's Dugout, Las Animas County, Colorado, date unknown

❦

The earliest schools of the Western Homestead Era were held in rude private dwellings wherein children from surrounding farms learned the basics under the volnuteer tutelage of an educated homesteader: a man or woman who somewhere "Back East" had gone clear through the eighth grade at least. Government had little or nothing to do with this schooling.

PLATE 9.

Homesteader's Dugout, Las Animas County, Colorado, date unknown

❧

The floor of this one-room dwelling, a typical west prairie "dugout," lies four feet below ground surface. Its upper walls are of pine logs cut in the canyons of the nearby Purgatoire, and skidded onto the prairie behind double horse teams. Its log walls are chinked with adobe, and its pole roof was covered with sod now grown over with cholla and other native plants.

Plate 10.

East Otto School, Union County, New Mexico, ca. 1910

❧

Outer dimensions of a typical, stone block or adobe south prairie school average 22 x 36 feet horizontally, 11 feet from ground surface to the tops of side and end walls, and 16 feet 5 inches from ground surface to the central ridge top of the hipped roof. Including plaster, the walls are 19 inches thick.

The classic south prairie schoolhouse has walls of adobe or native stone. Hidden in the folds of the prairie, this elegant example stands now a country mile from the nearest road of any kind. The two fledgling ravens, hatched in the attic, have been raised on emerging rattlesnakes whose winter den is under the floor.

PLATE 12.

Center Point School, Torrance County, New Mexico, ca. 1920

☙

On the arid southern prairies, subterranean, cement-lined cisterns, from whence the water was pumped by hand, were filled most reliably from water tanks on wheels. But here, an ingenious arrangement of gutters, downspout and concrete rainwater head replenished a cistern of five hundred gallons capacity.

PLATE 13.

Plum Valley School, Las Animas County, Colorado, ca. 1920

※

Many thousands of south prairie homesteads are now incorporated in big cattle ranches, and range cows, saddle horses, and wild pronghorns seek shelter in the shade of the abandoned schools. Over the years their pawing and tramping undermines the foundations, the walls fall outward and the schoolhouse is reduced to rubble.

PLATE 14.

Silvies School, Grant County, Oregon, ca. 1920

❦

Excluding the entryway, outer dimensions of the north prairie style averaged 20 x 30 feet horizontally, 11 feet 6 inches from ground surface to wall top, and 21 feet from ground surface to ridge top. The typical, hollow wall, made of wood and plaster, was 7 inches thick. The roof was not uncommonly adorned with a belfry.

PLATE 15.

Nine Mile School, Meade County, South Dakota, 1916

❧

The rather steeply pitched north prairie roof was made of unpainted, milled cedar shingles. The ridge was beaded with half-round galvanized tin. Siding was of pine clapboard painted white, and except for the unobtrusive chimney and eaves and the attractive entryway, attached external features were absent. The result was a pleasant, uncluttered structure of simple lines.

PLATE 16.

Typical North Prairie Schoolhouse Wall, Highland School,

Douglas County, Washington, ca. 1900

❧

Interior wall surfaces are of ½ inch of plaster over ½ x 2-inch laths nailed horizontally to the inner edges of the 2 x 4 studs. Exteriors are of clapboard on 1 x 12 shear paneling nailed diagonally to the outer edges of the 2 x 4s. The resulting, cold wall is seven inches thick, four inches of which is hollow center.

PLATE 17.

Eight Mile School, Morrow County, Oregon, 1882

☙

In the form of a single ceiling bulb, turned on and off with a dangling string, electricity first reached the prairie schoolhouse in the 1940s. Before then there was the coal oil (kerosene) lamp or two. But even after electricity arrived, schoolroom light was provided principally by one or another arrangement of tall windows.

PLATE 18.

North Middle Alkali School, Meade County, South Dakota, 1920

❧

Architectural embellishment was common among schools of the northern plains, and sometimes one or another adornment became popular over several thousand square miles. In western South Dakota, the north prairie style typically has a pedimented roof, a charming reminder of classical Greece brought here from New England and the Old South.

PLATE 19.

Dailey School, Park County, Montana, 1906

☙

The Dailey School is a north prairie classic in miniature. Its exterior horizontal dimensions measure only 16 x 24 feet. It was built by the rancher Dailey to provide an honest schoolhouse for the private education of his daughter. But children of neighboring homesteaders wanted to be included, so it soon became the Dailey Public School.

PLATE 20.

Lee School Number Two, Divide County, North Dakota, 1927

❦

Probably, Scandinavian homesteaders contributed more prairie schoolhouse variations than any other immigrant group. In western North Dakota it would seem that most Norwegian farmers were, in addition, carpenters and amateur architects, which commonly they were. This variant contains an interior "teacherage" which is all of five feet wide by eleven feet long.

PLATE 21.

Lee School Number One, Divide County, North Dakota, ca. 1915

☙

No two Norwegian one-room schools were alike. Each reflected the individual tastes and skills of farmers-cum-architects and contractors. Among these surviving school-houses are a seemingly endless variety of porches, attic windows, belfries, storm vest-ibules, and other decorative features, most of them having practical utility as well.

PLATE 22.

Moord School, Slope County, North Dakota, ca. 1910

☞

The pyramidal roof is absent from the southern plains and occurs in less than 2 percent of north prairie one-room schools. The peculiar, unsettling lines of this example, now a polling place, result from the removal of its belfry, which stood on the center-front of the main roof.

PLATE 23.

Carpenter School, Meade County, South Dakota, 1912

❧

Counterfeit stone block walls of poured concrete were expensive and time consuming, and were used rarely in one-room schools. The concrete was poured into a portable hand- and foot-powered machine which produced one block at a time, and whose molds could be ordered in a variety of styles, including "chiseled stone."

PLATE 24.

Depression School, Las Animas County, Colorado, ca. 1938

🖎

Interior trim reflected both taste and affordability. Beaded wainscoting of Pacific red cedar, topped with pine chair rails, was common both north and south, as in this adobe-walled school. In larger lengths this same beaded stock was sometimes used as ceiling material. One-half inch of commercial plaster covered both interior and exterior walls.

PLATE 25.

Trinity Lutheran (Public) School, Cheyenne County, Nebraska, ca. 1893

☙

Stamped tin ceilings were pricey and scarce. This ornate example dates to the building of Trinity Lutheran School in 1893, which eventually became Trinity Public School. The coved ceiling (the concave curve at the junction of ceiling and wall), whether of wood or tin, occurred in about 10 percent of north prairie schools.

PLATE 26.

Wild Rose School, Stark County, North Dakota, ca. 1910

☞

Nearly all of the homesteaders were of Christian heritage, and many were devout. Because government was seldom meddlesome, many a homesteaders' public schoolhouse had its religious expressions and uses. Thus, separation of church and state notwithstanding, this public school door testifies to the solid German Catholic population of School District 23.

PLATE 27.

Empire School, Meade County, South Dakota, 1915

☞

On the northern prairies the abandoned wood schoolhouses were frequently put to other uses (see Plates 22 and 30). The Empire School, with its original, rare pyramidal roof, is now a farmyard machine and repair shop. The metal sheathing, and the big, central roof vent have been added.

PLATE 28.

Cowan School, Park County, Montana, 1908

❧

The eccentric, nontypical Cowan School has two additional windows on its north side, and two more on its west-facing front. The walls, including the curious facade, are chiseled sandstone blocks in various hues and sizes, some of which weigh upwards of 200 pounds.

PLATE 29.

Lawn School, Box Butte County, Nebraska, 1930

❧

Another homely departure from the north prairie style, the Lawn School reflects the utilitarian experimentation of the 1920s and 1930s. Its walls are of hollow tile, and just as cold as those of wood. In addition to the west-facing front windows are four in the south wall. A basement doubles as a tornado shelter.

PLATE 30.

Lebo School, Meagher County, Montana, 1914

❧

In the late 1920s and early 1930s some north prairie states adopted the idea of the "Standard School." As in this example, with its window arrangements, interior rather than exterior storm vestibule, and other improvements, the Standard School was considered by bureaucrats to be state of the art. But most school districts declined to participate.

PLATE 31.

Lebo School, Meagher County, Montana, 1914

☙

"Standard School" or not, it was still a cold schoolhouse. In the 1930s and 1940s attempts to insulate north prairie hollow-walled schools involved drilling two-inch holes through the clapboard and filling the interior with rock wool, manufactured from molten slag or sedimentary rock, and blown in with a gasoline-powered machine.

PLATE 32.

Alpha School, Dawes County, Nebraska, ca. 1890

❧

Both north and south, prairie schoolhouse heating was provided most commonly by a potbellied stove. It burned either coal or wood, but because of the latter's scarcity on the prairies it was fueled nearly always with coal, mined in the Rockies, Black Hills, or Cascades. Note the typical teacher's platform behind this stove.

Plate 33.

Archuleta School, Las Animas County, Colorado, ca. 1911

℘

This was the standard schoolhouse door, distinguished by its five panels and its dimensions of about 32 x 80 inches. In the early 1900s it cost less than $2.00–delivered by rail to the nearest homestead town. Curiously, in this example, the doorknob assembly was mounted upside down.

PLATE 34.

The Girls' Room, Archuleta School, Las Animas County, Colorado, ca. 1911

☙

Schoolhouse privies combined decorum with the principles of sanitation. Boys' and girls' outhouses were placed well back of the schoolhouse, were separated usually by 100 feet or more, and were sited either at similar distances or downhill from the well or cistern. Their contents were treated frequently with quicklime.

Elk Vale School, Meade County, South Dakota, 1889

❦

During the years of President Franklin D. Roosevelt's New Deal, some of the classic prairie schoolhouse privies were replaced with up-to-date outhouses having trapdoor toilet lids, standpipe ventilators, screened windows, and poured concrete floors. This example is designed to accommodate both big boys and little boys.

PLATE 36.

Depression School, Las Animas County, Colorado, ca. 1934

❧

Typically, the schoolhouse had no teacherage. The teacher, usually a young, unmarried woman roomed and boarded with a nearby homestead family. Where a teacherage was provided, it was most commonly, as in this example, a small, shed-roofed rear annex containing a bedroom, and a combination living room and kitchen.

PLATE 37.

Teacherage, Pathfinder School, Cheyenne County, Nebraska, ca. 1908

≈

This nice example of a rare, detached teacherage has the basic lines of the classic, north prairie schoolhouse. Its single room contains 210 square feet of floor space and a useful storage attic. There is a single, east-facing door, and two small windows open to the north and south, respectively.

PLATE 38.

Teacher's Privy, Pathfinder School, Cheyenne County, Nebraska, ca. 1908

❧

Having one's own teacherage afforded privacy, but life without radio or neighbors could be lonely. By way of compensation the attractive little teacherage at Pathfinder School (see Plate 37) had a nice kitchen range, a "covered front porch," an attached combination bath and laundry room, and its own private outhouse.

PLATE 39.

Pony Barn, Malmborg School, Gallatin County, Montana, ca. 1890

☙

To come to school on horseback was to arrive with purpose. But in a northern winter there was the problem of how to shelter the horses once they got to school. The solution was the pony barn, where, during recess, the beloved steeds were groomed and sneaked lunch box apples.

Plate 40.

Cedar Hill School, Las Animas County, Colorado, 1938

℘

During the Great Depression President Franklin D. Roosevelt's Works Progress Administration (WPA) provided living wages for jobless artists and artisans. On the southern prairies, expert masons were put to work building or refurbishing rural schools, hence this fancy entrance with its door containing a salute to FDR.

PLATE 41.

"New" MacArthur School, Las Animas County, Colorado, 1938

❧

The expert, proud, and unemployed masons had plenty of time, and nothing else to do. The result was elaborate stone work, sometimes flamboyant, not always of critical utility, but provocative nevertheless. This fancy tunnel entrance may or may not have helped to keep tumbleweeds out of the schoolhouse.

PLATE 42.

"Old" MacArthur School, ca. 1900, and "New" MacArthur School,

Las Animas County, Colorado, 1938

☙

Many of the Works Progress Administration schoolhouses were unnecessary. Commonly, a perfectly adequate homemade school was abandoned or torn down, and an FDR schoolhouse was built beside it, or in its place. Be that as it may, the surviving WPA schools testify to the skills of their otherwise out-of-work artisans.

PLATE 43.

"New" MacArthur School, Las Animas County, Colorado, 1938

☙

While one may find the aesthetics of the WPA schools lacking as compared with their elegant homemade counterparts, WPA craftsmanship was impeccable. Imagine, in the typically uninspired modern public school, finding the sort of hand-tool perfection expressed here in chiseled exteriors, arched lintels, and even beaded mortar joints.

PLATE 44.

Prairie School Teacher, Colorado, 1934

❧

Teachers were trained at regional normal schools, two-year colleges designed especially to prepare their students for teaching grades one through eight, and whose curriculum offered both excellent training in the basics and instruction on how to handle prairie schoolchildren. Most of their graduates were young women, many of whom wound up marrying homesteaders.

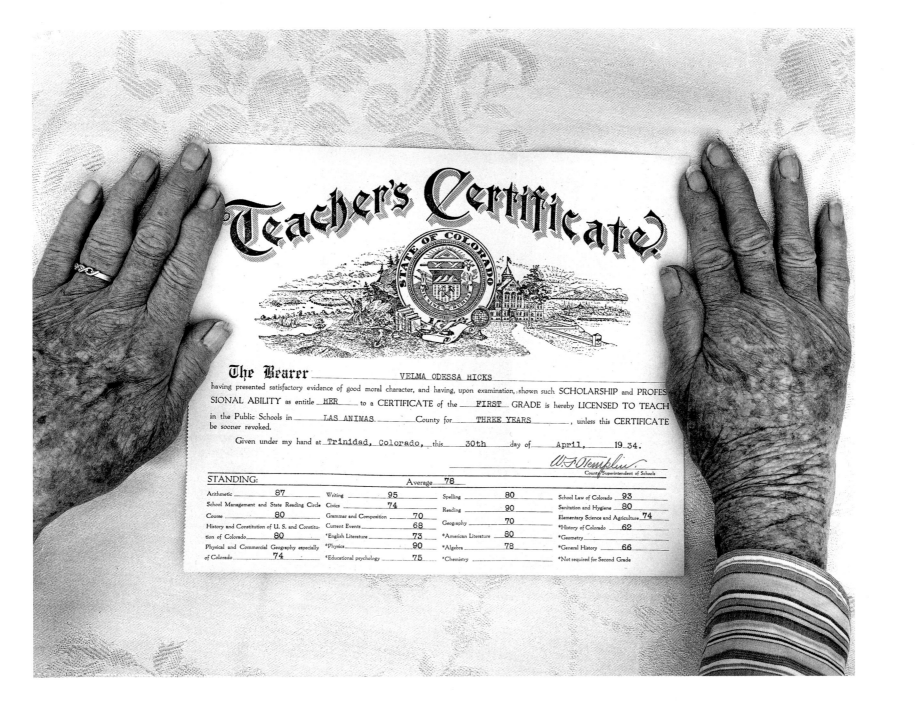

Teacher's Certificate

STATE OF COLORADO

The Bearer ___VELMA ODESSA HICKS___

having presented satisfactory evidence of good moral character, and having, upon examination, shown such SCHOLARSHIP and PROFESSIONAL ABILITY as entitle ___HER___ to a CERTIFICATE of the ___FIRST___ GRADE is hereby LICENSED TO TEACH in the Public Schools in ___LAS ANIMAS___ County for ___THREE YEARS___, unless this CERTIFICATE be sooner revoked.

Given under my hand at ___Trinidad, Colorado,___ this ___30th___ day of ___April,___ 19 _34._

W. F. Templin
County Superintendent of Schools

STANDING: Average ___78___

Arithmetic ___87___	Writing ___95___	Spelling ___80___	School Law of Colorado ___93___
School Management and State Reading Circle Course ___80___	Civics ___74___	Reading ___90___	Sanitation and Hygiene ___80___
History and Constitution of U. S. and Constitution of Colorado ___80___	Grammar and Composition ___70___	Geography ___70___	Elementary Science and Agriculture ___74___
	Current Events ___68___		*History of Colorado ___62___
Physical and Commercial Geography especially of Colorado ___74___	*English Literature ___73___	*American Literature ___80___	*Geometry _____
	*Physics ___90___	*Algebra ___78___	*General History ___66___
	*Educational psychology ___75___	*Chemistry _____	*Not required for Second Grade

PLATE 45.

Pathfinder School, Cheyenne County, Nebraska, ca. 1908

❧

The typical textbook contained study materials which covered several years of schooling. Thus, from the same book pupils of different grades studied simultaneously the same subject. Frequent—often daily—class recitation was required of each pupil in reading, spelling, and most other subjects, and penmanship was practiced every day.

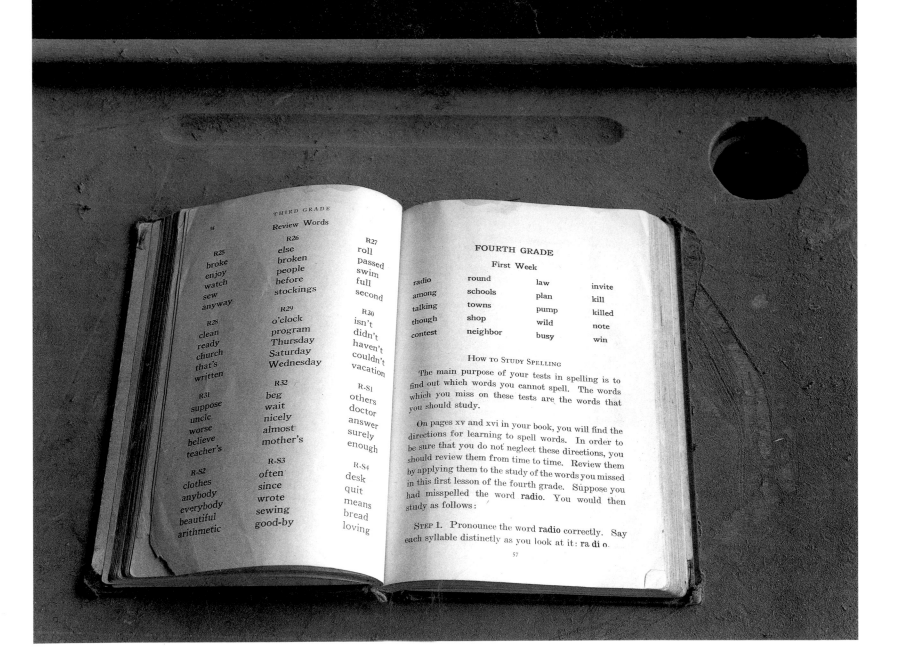

56

Review Words

R25
broke
enjoy
watch
sew
anyway

R26
else
broken
people
before
stockings

R27
roll
passed
swim
full
second

R28
clean
ready
church
that's
written

R29
o'clock
program
Thursday
Saturday
Wednesday

R30
isn't
didn't
haven't
couldn't
vacation

R31
suppose
uncle
worse
believe
teacher's

R32
beg
wait
nicely
almost
mother's

R-S1
others
doctor
answer
surely
enough

R-S2
clothes
anybody
everybody
beautiful
arithmetic

R-S3
often
since
wrote
sewing
good-by

R-S4
desk
quit
means
bread
loving

FOURTH GRADE

First Week

radio	round	law	invite
among	schools	plan	kill
talking	towns	pump	killed
though	shop	wild	note
contest	neighbor	busy	win

How to Study Spelling

The main purpose of your tests in spelling is to find out which words you cannot spell. The words which you miss on these tests are the words that you should study.

On pages xv and xvi in your book, you will find the directions for learning to spell words. In order to be sure that you do not neglect these directions, you should review them from time to time. Review them by applying them to the study of the words you missed in this first lesson of the fourth grade. Suppose you had misspelled the word **radio**. You would then study as follows:

STEP 1. Pronounce the word **radio** correctly. Say each syllable distinctly as you look at it: **ra di o**.

57

PLATE 46.

Pathfinder School, Cheyenne County, Nebraska, ca. 1908

☙

Today's attractive textbooks derive from these examples of the 1930s, when publishers in the increasingly lucrative school trade began turning out handsomely designed and illustrated texts. Usually, books were bought by parents or furnished by the school district, but dedicated teachers sometimes purchased a few favorites from their own meager salaries.

Shipley School, Stark County, North Dakota, 1908

❦

From the lowest grades, geography was among the most important subjects. The idea was simply that one could not understand the world and its events without knowing how it looked. Thus, every prairie schoolhouse was furnished with a wall case of large pull-down maps which covered the earth, including, of course, the school's home state.

CRAM'S IDEAL MAP OF NORTH DAKOTA

Published and Copyrighted by The George F. Cram Company; Indianapolis

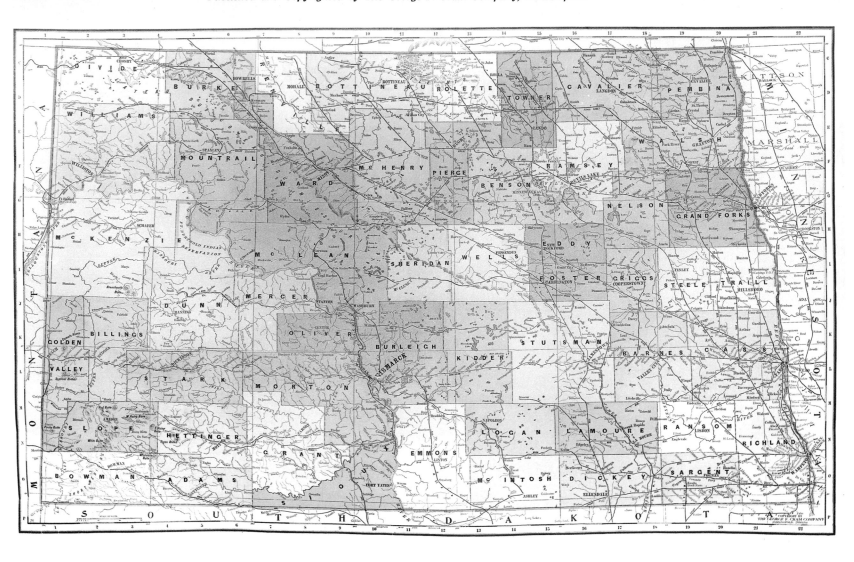

PLATE 48.

Idea School, Morrow County, Oregon, ca. 1885

❧

Teaching aids were scarce, and audio-visual was unheard of. But a common encouragement to concentration was a large framed print of Gilbert Charles Stuart's famous portrait of Washington, the one in which–no matter where you stand or sit–George Washington is looking at you.

PLATE 49.

Pathfinder School, Cheyenne County, Nebraska, ca. 1908

℘

Because of their increasing value as antiques, desks, bells, maps, and other furnishings have long since been taken from nearly all of the derelict prairie schools. Thus, in schoolhouse archaeology, this amazing find, with its marvelous artifacts, ranks with the discovery of King Tut's tomb. Note the archaeologists' footprints in the dust of the floor.

PLATE 50.

Alpha School, Dawes County, Nebraska, ca. 1890

☙

Penmanship was a universal part of the curriculum. Beginning in the lowest grades, pupils were taught the rolling style of the "Palmer Method." Upper graders were invited to send samples of their writing to the Palmer headquarters in Chicago, from which, if their work passed muster, they were mailed a certificate signed by Mr. Palmer himself.

l Mm Nn Oo Pp 2q

PLATE 51.

Half-Way School, Bighorn County, Montana, ca. 1905

☞

Keeping in mind that numerous pupils would not go on to further schooling, teachers designed a rather rigorous curriculum to provide a "solid education" to everyone who graduated from the eighth grade. As a testimonial to this achievement the Eighth Grade Diploma was often a wonderfully embellished, if somewhat busy, work of art.

Eighth Grade Diploma

This Certifies That

Vera Ernestine Cleland

has satisfactorily completed the Course of Study prescribed for the Eighth Grade of the Montana Public Schools and is entitled to

Admission to the High School Department

Given at Hardin, Montana, this 7th day of June 1915

C. Bernice Myers
Harry G. Rogers
Sarah F. Dakin

County Board of Examiners

W. M. WELCH DIPLOMA HOUSE, CHICAGO.

PLATE 52.

Villegreen School, Las Animas County, Colorado, ca. 1915

☙

On the homestead frontier, any piano was a rare luxury (although to grace parlors and saloons some are known to have been carried hundreds of miles in horse drawn wagons). A schoolhouse piano was rarer still. This upright was donated by a music-loving homestead lady with family money from back east.

PLATE 53.

Roundabout, Sedan School, Gallatin County, Montana, 1920

☙

Each school yard contained a small array of potentially dangerous recreational equipment. When well greased, the common roundabout (merry-go-round) could be made to revolve at amazing speed. Hence the addition to this example of the extra, iron handholds, designed to keep dizzy passengers from being flung off in all directions.

PLATE 54.

Sedan School, Gallatin County, Montana, 1920

❧

Hardly a school yard was without its slide, which was even more common than the roundabout, and somewhat less likely to produce concussions and dislocations. Nevertheless, as a primary grader, on a good, tall well-polished slide, until you learned to hit the ground running, you collected your share of cuts and abrasions.

PLATE 55.

Consolidated School, Lucy, New Mexico, ca. 1910

❧

Bringing pupils into town awaited the advent of "all weather" dirt and gravel roads. This concrete-walled consolidated school contained four classrooms, four teachers, and more than a hundred students. But for the past fifty years, Mr. and Mrs. A. T. Formwalt have been the sole inhabitants of the homestead town of Lucy.

PLATE 56.

Homestead House, Harney County, Oregon, ca. 1910

❧

The big sage country ruined more homesteaders more quickly than did any other part of the western homestead lands. Despite their promise, the sagebrush plains proved just too dry to farm. In eastern Oregon, between 1910 and 1915, tens of thousands of acres of sagebrush were plowed under, planted to corn, wheat, and even peaches–and then abandoned.

PLATE 57.

Homestead Outbuildings, Lander County, Nevada, ca. 1915

☙

Practically speaking, homesteading in Nevada was a total failure. Nevada, from one end to the other, is desert pure and simple. Still, some homesteaders tried. Before they gave up finally, this homestead family built a system of dams, dikes, and ditches with the forlorn hope of channeling desert cloudbursts to their fields.

PLATE 58.

East Otto School, Union County, New Mexico, ca. 1910

❧

The ravages of the Dust Bowl were awesome. Today, in eastern New Mexico, homesteaders' abandoned fields remain as sunken rectangles, their topsoil heaped five feet
high along the enclosing fence lines. The dry winds obliterated the surface of this school
yard, exposing the base of the school's foundation and the lower neck of the cistern.

PLATE 59.

Homestead House, Union County, New Mexico, date unknown

☙

In the big New Mexico counties which border on Texas and Oklahoma, thousands of elegant prairie dwellings were abandoned. The thick, adobe walls, and the tall, low windows of this five-room house reflect the Spanish-Mexican Southwest. The bull's-eye molding is derived, most directly, from the eastern United States.

PLATE 60.

Highland School, Douglas County, Washington, ca. 1900

❧

If you like friendly people, and if you want to learn firsthand about the last, big chapter in the opening of the West, then come out to the shortgrass plains and the big sage country; eat canned peaches and drink coffee with canned milk in it, and listen while the old survivors tell the story of the prairie schoolhouse.

Bibliography

Allen, Barbara. *Homesteading the High Desert*. Salt Lake City: University of Utah Press, 1987.

Anonymous. "Yesterday's Challenge." *The Wichita Eagle* [Wichita, Kansas], Op-Ed page, November 17, 1991.

Billington, Ray Allen. *America's Frontier Heritage*. Albuquerque: University of New Mexico Press, 1974.

Blumenson, John J.-G. *Identifying American Architecture: A Pictorial Guide to Styles and Terms, 1600–1945*. New York: W. W. Norton & Company, 1981.

Daniels, Darwin. *If The West Wind Could Speak*. Wagon Mound, N.M.: Santa Fe Trails Publishing Company, 1992.

Dick, Everett. *The Sod House Frontier*. Lincoln: University of Nebraska Press, 1979.

Ferguson, Denzel, and Nancy Ferguson. *Oregon's Great Basin Country*. Bend, Ore.: Maverick Publications, 1982.

Fleming, John, Hugh Honour, and Nikolaus Pevsner. *The Penguin Dictionary of Architecture*. Middlesex, England: Penguin Books Ltd, 1980.

Gates, Paul W. *History of Public Land Development*. New York: Arno Press, 1979.

Gillette, J. M. "Study of Population Trends in North Dakota." *North Dakota Historical Quarterly* 9, no. 3 (1942): 179–93.

Gulliford, Andrew. *America's Country Schools*. Washington, D.C.: Preservation Press, 1984.

Hargreaves, Mary W. M. *Dry Farming in the Northern Great Plains, 1900–1925*. Cambridge, Mass.: Harvard University Press, 1957.

———. *Dry Farming in the Northern Great Plains: Years of Readjustment 1920–1990*. Lawrence: University Press of Kansas, 1993.

Hatton, Raymond R. *High Desert of Central Oregon*. Portland, Ore.: Binford and Mort, 1981.

Houghton, Samuel G. *A Trace of Desert Waters: The Great Basin Story*. Salt Lake City: Howe Brothers, 1986.

Hubbard, Horace Benjamin. *A History of the Public Land Policies*. Madison: University of Wisconsin Press, 1965.

Kraenzel, Carl. *The Great Plains In Transition*. Norman: University of Oklahoma Press, 1955.

Lindgren, H. Elaine. *Land In Her Own Name*. Fargo: North Dakota Institute of Regional Studies, 1991.

Rankin, Dorothy, ed. *Country School Legacy: Humanities on the Frontier*. Silt: Colo.: Country School Legacy, 1981.

Rölvaag, O. E. *Giants in the Earth*. New York: Harper and Row, 1955.

Sandoz, Mari. *Old Jules*. Boston: Little, Brown and Company, 1935.

Schroeder, Joseph J., Jr., ed. *1908 Sears, Roebuck Catalogue: A Treasured Replica from the Archives of History*. Northfield, Ill.: Digest Books, 1971.

Scott, John S. *The Penguin Dictionary of Building*. Middlesex, England: Penguin Books Ltd., 1987.

Webb, Walter Prescott. *The Great Plains*. Lincoln: University of Nebraska Press, 1981.

150

THE PRAIRIE SCHOOLHOUSE

Edited by Dana Asbury

Composed in Baskerville using Quark XPress, version 3.3 for Windows

Text film output by Integrated Composition Systems, Spokane, Washington

Duotone separations, printing, and binding by Sung-In Printing America, Inc.

Text printed on 120 gsm Velvet Art

Designed by Kristina Kachele

Printed in Korea